SAFE & SOUND

Social Media

Paul J. Larson, M.Ed.

Consultants

Timothy Rasinski, Ph.D.
Kent State University

Lori Oczkus, M.A.
Literacy Consultant

Olivia Applegate
Crime Prevention Specialist
Chino Police Department

Publishing Credits

Rachelle Cracchiolo, M.S.Ed., *Publisher*
Conni Medina, M.A.Ed., *Managing Editor*
Dona Herweck Rice, *Series Developer*
Emily R. Smith, M.A.Ed., *Content Director*
Stephanie Bernard/Noelle Cristea, M.A.Ed., *Editors*
Robin Erickson, *Senior Graphic Designer*

The TIME logo is a registered trademark of TIME Inc. Used under license.

Image Credits: p.5 Catchlight Visual Services/Alamy Stock Photo; p.14 Jiangang Wang/Getty Images; p.22 akindo/Getty Images; p.26 Don Farrall/Getty Images; p.28 Justin Paget/Getty Images; p.34 Richard Stonehouse/Getty Images; pp.34–35 Michael Short/Bloomberg via Getty Images; pp.40–41 Gavin Roberts/PC Plus Magazine via Getty Images; all other images from iStock and/or Shutterstock

3 2121 00073 4554

Teacher Created Materials

5301 Oceanus Drive
Huntington Beach, CA 92649-1030
http://www.tcmpub.com
ISBN 978-1-4938-3628-4
© 2017 Teacher Created Materials, Inc.

Table of Contents

What Is Social Media?. 4

Social Media Origins 6

Text, Image, Video, and More 10

How Can It Help You?. 14

How Can It Hurt You? 18

What about Cyberbullying?. 28

Navigating Social Media 34

From Exclusive to Universal 42

Glossary 44

Index. 45

Check It Out! 46

Try It!. 47

About the Author 48

What Is Social Media?

Flash back to the 1990s: Cell phones are the size of pencil boxes. Most computers are small fortresses and firmly housed on desktops. Laptops? They are lighter than their desktop counterparts, yes, but finding and connecting to a wireless system is a difficult task. And social media? The notion doesn't even exist.

What we consider social media today includes the collection of applications and websites that people use to share information and to connect with others. The ability to make these connections is based on the Internet.

When the Internet was developing in the 1990s, online access was moving from large institutions to home computers. People accessed the Internet via their home telephone lines. **Dial-up** was the way to get online. America Online® (AOL®) and CompuServe® were the biggest **Internet service providers** (ISPs) of the time.

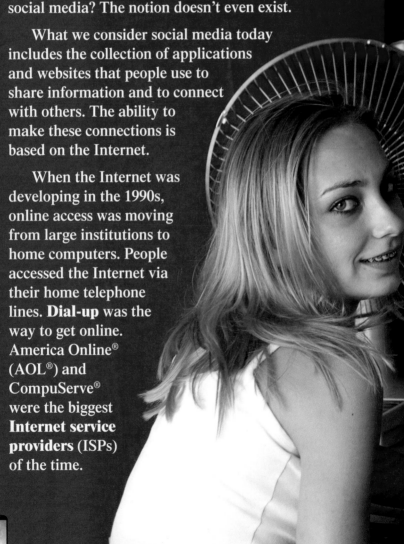

Who Said That?

Tina Sharkey claims that she was the person who coined the term "social media" while working at AOL on iVillage®, a media company that launched in 1995. Here's her story: "I said, 'Well, it's not like service media, and it's not quite informational media—it's social media!'" She even owns the domain socialmedia.com. However, it wasn't registered until 1999, and therefore there is no solid evidence she created the term.

Who Was *Really* First?

Two other people claim to have coined the term "social media." In 1995, Darrell Berry wrote a paper using the term "social media spaces" to describe the Internet as a network of people communicating with each other. Ted Leonsis, an executive at AOL in 1997, wanted users to have "social media, places where they can be entertained, communicate, and participate in a social environment."

Social Media Origins

The inventions of the movable-type printing press, the telephone, the radio, and the computer caused **paradigm shifts** in the technological world. But the rapid spread of the Internet changed the world of communication like nothing before.

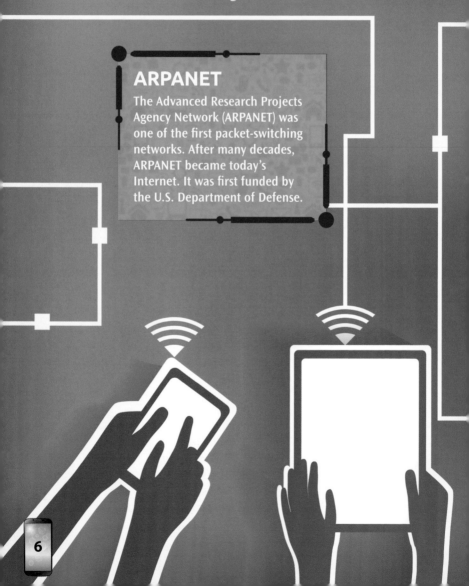

ARPANET

The Advanced Research Projects Agency Network (ARPANET) was one of the first packet-switching networks. After many decades, ARPANET became today's Internet. It was first funded by the U.S. Department of Defense.

The Internet

But what exactly *is* the Internet? It serves as a quick means of communication between groups of computers. The computers use a technique called *packet switching*. In a nutshell, this breaks down a large message into many smaller messages called *packets*. The packets are then transmitted and can be shared by multiple users at the same time. Governments, businesses, and educational institutions loved this new system from its onset! To put it simply, the Internet is a way for almost all computers in the world to connect.

The First Message

In October 1969, ARPANET sent its first electronic message. A student at the University of California, Los Angeles was trying to send the word *login* as a message to people at Stanford University; the University of California, Santa Barbara; and the University of Utah. The funny thing is, after sending the letters *l* and *o*, the system crashed! Engineers corrected the problem and were able to send the entire message an hour later.

The Information Age

Not only did ARPANET lay the foundation for the Internet, but it also ushered in what we know as the Information Age. The technology of the 1970s and '80s brought new options to people in the '90s. Personal computers moved from the drawing board into people's homes. Word processing and spreadsheet programs were now at the fingertips of new computer users. The world was again ready for the next big thing.

The 1990s brought us many new business, learning, and research opportunities as well as new forms of entertainment. People could communicate with each other almost instantly via email—even from across the world. **Floppy disks** and CD-ROMs (commonly called CDs) became the preferred devices for storing vast amounts of information.

Floppy Disks

Early computers did not have USB ports or CD-ROM drives. Instead, floppy disks were the way to install new programs onto computers or to back up information. Since most programs were larger than 1.44 MB (the capacity of one floppy disk), multiple disks were required to install programs.

Compact Disc Read-Only Memory

When the CD-ROM emerged on the market, it quickly became popular because it had a much larger capacity than the floppy disk did. You might think this pushed floppy disks into the backs of desk drawers to be forgotten. But unlike a floppy disk, a CD-ROM is "read only," as indicated in the name. That means you can see the information it contains, but you can't change it or add new information. So users still required a way to save and transport files. Today, there are much smaller devices used for storage—USB flash drives.

But the Internet remained at the heart of these changes. There had to be a way to store and share information not only on floppy disks and CD-ROMs but also in **cyberspace**. Was there a way to use the Internet to aid in collecting and organizing information? And how did this lead to the development of social media?

Text, Image, Video, and More

By the end of the 1990s, millions of people worldwide were using the Internet. Many people could connect through ISPs 24 hours a day to search, retrieve, and save information with just a few clicks of a mouse. But even so, the public wanted more. Users wanted to know what kinds of experiences others were having and what others were doing with their lives. Was there a way they could share their experiences? Indeed, there was.

Bulletin Board Systems

One online meeting place, called a **bulletin board system** (BBS), gave users the freedom to not only download files and games, but also post messages to other users. BBSs were usually technology related.

The downside of BBSs was that users frequently had to deal with long-distance calling fees, which quickly became very expensive. Because of the expenses involved for users, many bulletin boards became locally based. That allowed groups of BBS users to go to local in-person gatherings. Just like that, the techies who had likely worked alone up to this point became connected to other like-minded individuals.

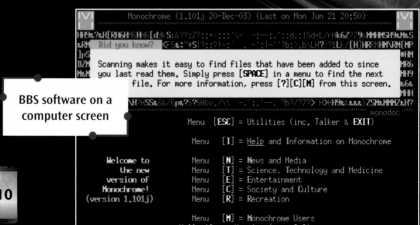

BBS software on a computer screen

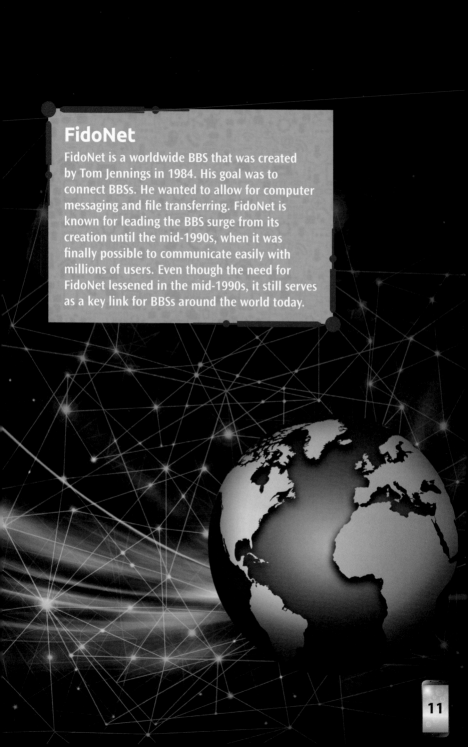

FidoNet

FidoNet is a worldwide BBS that was created by Tom Jennings in 1984. His goal was to connect BBSs. He wanted to allow for computer messaging and file transferring. FidoNet is known for leading the BBS surge from its creation until the mid-1990s, when it was finally possible to communicate easily with millions of users. Even though the need for FidoNet lessened in the mid-1990s, it still serves as a key link for BBSs around the world today.

Chat Rooms

Another text-based social media form of the 1990s was the **chat room**. Chat rooms were first introduced in 1988 by Internet Relay Chat (IRC). This was a collection of networks that allowed people to "chat" about a variety of topics, share links, and offer technical assistance to one another.

ISPs helped the popularity of chat rooms grow. By 1997, AOL was hosting over 19,000 chat rooms. With an increase in new users, chat rooms grew in popularity. In fact, AOL users spent more than one million hours combined in chat rooms every day. Chat rooms made it possible for users to have conversations with people all over the world without ever leaving the comfort of their homes.

eWorld

When ISPs still dominated the online world, Apple created a subscription-based service for Mac users: eWorld. When logged in, a user could visit a virtual city. Each of the buildings in the city represented a different topic and contained articles, chat rooms, discussion boards, and downloadable files.

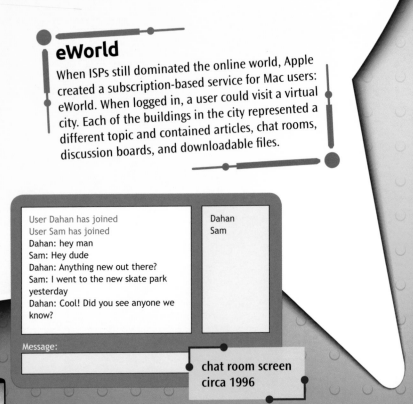

User Dahan has joined
User Sam has joined
Dahan: hey man
Sam: Hey dude
Dahan: Anything new out there?
Sam: I went to the new skate park yesterday
Dahan: Cool! Did you see anyone we know?

Dahan
Sam

Message:

chat room screen circa 1996

STOP! THINK...

Based on the graphs below, it's clear that overall IRC usage has declined steadily for years. In fact, IRCs lost 60 percent of their users in just one decade. That's a huge fall in numbers for any kind of service!

- To what do you attribute this steady decline?
- How would you describe the correlation between the two graphs?
- If you were an investor today, would you be more likely to invest in an IRC site or a social networking site? Why?

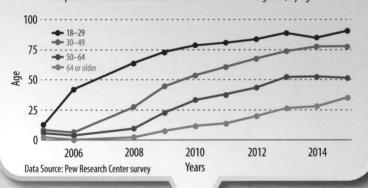

The percent of American adults who use social newtorking sites, by age

- 18–29
- 30–49
- 50–64
- 64 or older

Data Source: Pew Research Center survey

Years

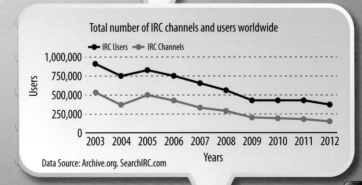

Total number of IRC channels and users worldwide

- IRC Users
- IRC Channels

Data Source: Archive.org. SearchIRC.com

Years

How Can It Help You?

Connecting to the Internet and to social media sites provides people with a broad range of opportunities. Social connections can be built and maintained through those sites. People can even find new jobs on social media. For example, LinkedIn® networking services helps people connect to other professionals and find new career paths. Add in the ability to access information with just a few clicks, and life is good! Using text messages, images, and audio files to share thoughts, feelings, and information has never been easier.

In fact, even those who run companies and businesses take to social media. It's been used to promote sales, new locations, or any information they want quickly shared with the public. Social media has become a large part of everyday life, and business owners know it's a great way to spread worthwhile information. There is no doubt that social media can be a very powerful tool.

As you investigate the benefits of social media, put yourself in the center of the picture.

◎ How does communication via social media compare with communication in the real world?

◎ What do you see as social media's greatest benefit?

Social Media Explained with Hot Chocolate

Having trouble keeping track of what each social media site is for? Here's an easy way to remember:

Facebook®: React to my post about hot chocolate.

YouTube®: Watch me sip my hot chocolate!

Twitter®: I'm drinking my hot chocolate right now.

Instagram®: Here's a photo of hot chocolate in my favorite mug.

Snapchat®: Look at my hot chocolate photo before it disappears.

Tumblr®: Here's a little story about my love of hot chocolate.

Pinterest®: Here's a recipe for delicious hot chocolate.

Social Media and Teens

Since the creation of social media sites, online activity has grown significantly. There are scores of popular social media sites and apps. They offer a wide variety of communication modes. In fact, they have become an integral part of our daily lives. But at what cost?

Some experts claim that the modified language used on social media sites has led to the decline in social and communication skills of kids and teens. Others, however, find that social networking services play a vital role for teens. Social media delivers information, promotes supportive relationships, and can even create a sense of belonging.

YL!

BRE

TBH

LOL

More Text Lingo

Many teens are experts in "textspeak," the way people write in text messages. Here are four keys to using textspeak:

1. Use homophones instead of words ("b4" for "before" or "gr8" for "great").
2. Leave some letters out of words ("wud" for "would").
3. Abbreviate phrases (such as "LOL" for "laugh out loud" or "BTW" for "by the way").
4. Leave out the punctuation altogether.

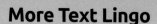

How Can It Hurt You?

You might think that you have a good understanding of all the social media dangers and how to steer clear of them. But it's vital to remember this: Internet safety is only one part of what it takes to recognize the potential dangers of social media.

What about the Children?

Children younger than 13 should be supervised when using the Internet. Social media networks have minimum age requirements to keep children safe. So it's important for everyone, regardless of age, to be careful. Be sure you're not posting too much about yourself. For instance, there is *never* a good reason to share personal addresses. Don't post pictures of the exterior of anyone's house on a social media site. It's important to protect your privacy on social media, as **predators** wait for the right opportunities to take advantage.

Just as a child may attempt to fake his or her age online to create a profile, potential predators can just as easily create fictitious profiles, claiming to be about the same age and interested in the same things as their targets. These people make a habit of luring kids and teens into a false sense of security, all the while devising hurtful plans. Make sure you are aware of how much you're revealing about yourself on any social media site.

Where Is Everybody?

About 92 percent of American teens between the ages of 13 and 17 use social media every day. That is the main reason predators focus on social media sites and apps.

How Old Are You?

Virtually every social media site has a minimum age requirement. Twitter's is buried in its **privacy policy**, but others, such as Facebook, ask for age verification when signing up for an account. Here are requirements for some of the most popular sites:

AGE
RESTRICTIONS
FOR SOCIAL
MEDIA
PLATFORMS

13
Twitter
Facebook
Instagram
Pinterest
Google+®
Tumblr
Reddit®
Snapchat

14 LinkedIn

16 WhatsApp®

18 Path®

18 YouTube, WeChat®,
or 13 with Foursquare®, Flickr®
parent permission

Avoiding the Scam Jam

The presence of **scammers** is another unfortunate byproduct of social media. Much like pickpockets, these individuals gravitate toward large crowds. With more than 90 percent of teens on social media networks, these thieves are finding more targets than ever!

Phishing

There are some scammers who would like to have your personal information. They instigate clever and convincing attempts to steal that information so that they can commit identity theft or fraud. These scammers are **phishing**. The thieves create websites that appear to be your favorite networks and work to manipulate you into visiting their sites. They do this with the intent of stealing your password. Once a scammer has your password, the real trouble begins.

With your password, a scammer has the ability to take over your real profiles or create fictitious accounts using your information. These untrustworthy people may send out **spam** messages and **viruses**, which would have negative impacts on the friends in your networks.

Shady Contests

Some scammers lure teens into their schemes with contests promising unbelievable results. These scammers are usually phishing for your personal information, which is typically asked for on the application. Beware of these types of scams!

Unsavory Scholarships

Another strategy used by scammers to attract teens is advertising fake grants or scholarships. Their applications often ask for personal information, such as a home address, parents' credit card numbers, and even Social Security numbers. When applying for grants or scholarships, make sure they are from accredited and trusted institutions.

Photographs

Many people love to share their photos on social media. Scrolling through your news feed, you can find countless selfies. There are also people who love to share the great times they're having with friends through photos of the activities or by "checking in" to different locations. But many people may not want their images or information plastered all over the Internet. Try developing a good habit: before posting a friend's image or checking him or her in, ask for their approval.

The problem with photographs is that once they are posted, they become a part of the social media landscape forever. Even if the posting is only up for a moment and then removed—as with Snapchat—there may be a person who sees it and screenshots the image. It's not uncommon for photos to **go viral** and make people laugh. But to the person or people in the photos, it might cause shame, embarrassment, or even the loss of a job.

Social Media Faux Pas

According to a recent survey conducted by On Device Research, 1 in 10 people aged 16 to 34 have been passed over for a job because of something they have posted on a social media website.

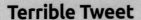

Terrible Tweet

Twitter is a powerful social media site. It is widely used, but not everyone realizes the potential problems social media could cause.

In 2015, a teen found herself out of work before she even started her first day at her job. The day before beginning work at a pizza parlor, she complained on Twitter about having to start work the next day! Bad idea. Her new boss saw her tweet and tweeted back that she didn't have to bother showing up because she was fired.

Another problem with sharing photos and images is **copyright infringement**. You may find a photograph or image that you like very much. You should check to see you need permission before posting it. The copyright symbol © on any photo or image guarantees that you must ask before using it.

As for written materials, you will often find the following statement: "No part of this text may be reproduced, stored in, introduced into a retrieval system, transmitted in any form by any means." If you see this, it means you have to ask permission before using it *any* reason.

Anything that someone else has created is known as *work*. It is that person's intellectual property. Copyright owners have the rights to their intellectual property that person's life plus 70 more years. If you use copyrighted material or images owned by a person, you may have to pay **civil damages** to that person.

Punishing Plagiarism

Plagiarism is a dangerous business and may have devastating consequences. You often hear about it in schoolwork, but here is another example:

In 2014, John Walsh, a U.S. senator from Montana, had his master's degree stripped away after it was discovered he had plagiarized part of his final paper in 2007. In its 14 pages, at least 25 percent of the information appeared to have been taken from other people's work. A month after the information was revealed, he pulled the plug on his reelection campaign.

What Is a Copyright?

According to the United States Copyright Office, *copyright* is defined as "a form of intellectual property law" that "protects original works of authorship including literary, dramatic, musical, and artistic works, such as poetry, novels, movies, songs, computer software, and architecture. Copyright does not protect facts, ideas, systems, or methods of operation, although it may protect the way these things are expressed."

Q&A

with Olivia Applegate

Crime Prevention Specialist of the Chino Police Department in California

How is the Crime Prevention Unit involved with social media?

The Chino Police Department Crime Prevention Unit is proactively participating in the education of social media safety. With constantly evolving social media outlets, it is crucial to make the public aware of the possible dangers before engagement. People can access the Internet through many different types of sites. They can post photos, share information, and communicate freely. It is important to accept "friends" and "followers" only if the user personally knows them. When creating a profile, it is crucial not to provide personal information. That may include your address, telephone number, current location, etc. These steps can help prevent potential victimization.

Protect
Security

Password

What would your key recommendation be for a young person preparing to join a social media site?

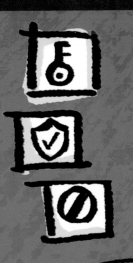

When providing prevention education to teens with regard to social media sites, always remember the four Rs.

- **Recognize** techniques used by online predators to deceive their victims.

- **Refuse** requests for personal information.

- **Respond** assertively if you are ever in an uncomfortable situation while online.

- **Report** to a parent or other trusted adult any suspicious or dangerous contact that makes you uncomfortable.

PROTECTION ☑

DATA

LOCK!

What about Cyberbullying?

Unfortunately bullies have tarnished society since the start of civilization. The newest problem is this: technology. It has given bullies a whole new landscape in which to pick on and harm others. Name calling and trash talking—both virtually and in the real world—can have disastrous effects on young people.

Bad Intentions

Cyberbullying happens when the Internet is used to harass peers and most commonly occurs among young people. Cyberbullying can sometimes be easy to recognize. For example, if anyone receives a tweet, text, or response on a social network platform that is cruel, vulgar, or mean and is directed at them specifically, that is cyberbullying.

Take the First Step

One of the first things you can do when you are dealing with a cyberbully is to sign off the site where they are bothering you. Try to stay calm, collect your thoughts, and avoid reacting out of hurt or anger. Acting on these emotions can lead to poor choices. And that means you could say something that might make the situation worse or could get you in trouble yourself.

At other times, it might not be as obvious. For example, someone pretending to be you online could lead to trouble. Or a person may post your personal information or photos and videos that could embarrass or hurt you. These are all examples of cyberbullying. There have even been reports of online accounts being created specifically just to harass or bully people.

Fakes

One day you may receive a friend request from someone you're already friends with. Don't fall for it! Most likely it is someone trying to impersonate your *real* friend. Be sure to report any suspicious requests like these.

Unintended Outcomes

Surprisingly, a person may become a cyberbully without realizing it. Text messages, emails, and tweets don't always come across as clearly as you might think. Just because you read it one way, doesn't mean that another person will read it in the same way. Words, phrases, and even **emoji** can sometimes be misinterpreted. This means that one person's joke may unintentionally come across as an insult to someone else. So how can you tell if the bullying is intentional? A pattern of repeated texts, emails, and posts are more than likely *not* accidental.

A Constant Problem

Unfortunately, this type of bullying has become a full-time problem. Unlike in-person bullying, cyberbullying can happen at any time. Text messages can be sent at any time of the day, and the Internet is always available. For people who are victimized, they might have a sense that the harassment is unending. As long as people keep using digital devices, the risk of cyberbullying will always be present.

Print it Out

If a cyberbully continues to bother you, you may want to print the messages or screenshots. Then, you can share them with a trusted adult who has the skills to help you. In this way, you are not "tattling" but standing up for yourself.

Block That Bully

If someone bullies you with texts or on a social media site, you can delete that person from your contacts or friends list. If they are sending you a lot of hurtful texts, you can block them from your account or block the bully's phone number. This way, you will not have to see any of their messages.

Types of Cyberbullying

Even though cyberbullying is a somewhat recent phenomenon, it's evident that its effects can last a long time. Victims of cyberbullying, much like victims of physical bullies, can experience mental and emotional strain, depression, anxiety, anger, and even suicidal tendencies.

According to research, the most common examples of cyberbullying include:

- **exclusion:** when a person purposely **blacklists** someone from a group, then taunts him or her
- **flaming:** when a person uses vulgar or inappropriate language to attack or fight with someone online
- **harassing:** when a person continually sends inappropriate, hurtful, or even hateful messages to someone online
- **impersonation:** when a person poses as someone else to ruin his or her reputation
- **outing:** when a person shares a victim's personal information or secrets on a social media site
- **stalking:** when a person "follows" another person online and sends him or her messages with the intention of hurting, scaring, intimidating, or simply ignoring personal boundaries

Navigating Social Media

As you grow older, you develop a desire to share more of your opinions and ideas. Social media is one place where debating and discussion skills can develop. Whether talking to friends or weighing in on important topics, teens work on different ways of presenting themselves. A social network can be a place to create, cultivate, and strengthen friendships. The wide variety of social media gives you and others opportunities to experience socializing in virtual communities. In doing so, you can create your own unique voice. But, as is said, "With great power there must also come great responsibility." Always think about what you're going to post so it can't come back to haunt you!

Education over Social Media

Malala Yousafzai, a Nobel Prize–winning Pakistani, was shot by the Taliban at the age of 15 for pursuing an education. When asked in an interview with the *New York Times* about social media, she responded, "I haven't gotten on Twitter or Facebook yet because I want to focus on my education."

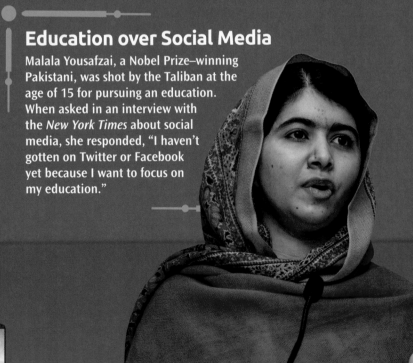

Creating an Identity

When asked about what people do on his social media site, Mark Zuckerberg, the founder of Facebook, said, "They're keeping up with their friends and family, but they're also building an image and identity for themselves. They're connecting with the audience that they want to connect to."

Protecting Yourself

Staying safe on social media is not just a good idea, it is **imperative**. Social media networks are innovative ways to keep in touch with people and share thoughts, photos, and links with friends and family. However, there are also predators, scammers, and cyberbullies lurking on those same sites with the intent of carrying out harmful deeds. So, what are some steps you can take to protect yourself?

First, it's vital to remember that the Internet is forever. Once you've posted a message, a photograph, or a video, it's out there—even if you delete the post or the entire account. You never know who may have seen or copied it.

Lesson: Be mindful about what you post.

Second, be aware of who your online or social media "friends" are—if you don't know a person in real life, then you probably shouldn't accept them as a friend on social media, as this opens the door for potential predators or scammers. When it comes to the ever-growing world of cyberspace, you never know exactly what someone's intentions may be.

Lesson: Only accept a friend request online if it's from someone you know in the real world.

THINK LINK

◎ What would you do if a stranger repeatedly approached you on a social media site or app?

◎ Imagine you're helping someone younger than you to create his or her first profile. What information should be included, and what should be left out? Why?

Third, be cautious when you click on links—even if friends or family shared them. A friend's account may have been taken over by a scammer and the link could be corrupt. Corrupted links contain viruses or **worms** that damage operating systems. You certainly don't want something like that infecting your computer or device. Before clicking, be sure that the link goes to a reliable site—either one that you're familiar with or that has a trusted domain, such as .edu, .gov, or .org. Also, when you are browsing a site and feel enticed to click a pop-up for an unbelievable deal or easy contest that seems too good to be true, don't click it! It's probably exactly what it seems: too good to be true. Giveaways, easy wins, and remarkable deals on social media are seldom as great as they seem.

Lesson: Think before you click.

Fourth, consider the privacy of your posts and your accounts. When you create a social media page or account, you have the option of editing the privacy settings. Take the initiative and ensure that you only share information with family and friends. Establishing a protocol, or system, to review your privacy settings once a month would be ideal.

Lesson: Keep your private life private.

Koobface

There are types of **malware** that infect not only specific devices but also the networks they share with other devices. One such worm is Koobface. Its first targets were social network sites such as Facebook and Twitter. How did it enter people's system? When they clicked on deceiving links!

39

Fifth, keep your personal information confidential. You have every right to be suspicious of anyone on a social media site who requests personal information of any kind. Be smart—refrain from sharing your phone number, address, or other identifying information.

Lesson: Not everyone is trustworthy. If you don't know a person, don't share your personal information.

Finally, be sure to use different passwords for each site or account. It may be easier to use the same password over and over again, but the problem is if someone were to discover the password, he or she would have access to all the sites and accounts where you use it. So take some time to create new passwords for all sites or accounts. Be sure that new passwords contain combinations of letters and numbers and are at least eight characters in length. It is also helpful to change your passwords periodically to keep things secure.

Lesson: Use different passwords and update them frequently.

Password Safety

Today there are many apps, such as LastPass, that can generate strong passwords and store your login information securely!

From Exclusive to Universal

The realm of social media has grown considerably over the past few decades. From starting with an extremely limited online experience to allowing millions of people to use sites and apps every single day, social media has come a long way. Add in the explosion of mobile devices, such as smart phones and tablets, and it's easy to see why social media has found its way into nearly every aspect of our lives.

Whether you are an everyday user of multiple social media sites or you are just creating your first account, the key is to remain safe. And the best way to do that is to use, and trust, your common sense. Be mindful with whom you are sharing your personal information. Become aware of the sites you shouldn't visit. And always stay cautious in your online conversations. Doing these things will keep you safe and sound in your social media adventures.

The Next Big Thing

The popularity of social media platforms consistently changes. Popular social media sites and apps have taken over how people interact with each other, and it's hard to find a young person now who isn't part of the social media world. What will be the next big platform? One can only guess!

Glossary

blacklists—puts someone onto a list of people to be avoided

bulletin board system—a computer application for exchanging messages and files

chat room—virtual room where a chat session takes place among multiple participants

civil damages—money given to the winner of a court case

copyright infringement—using works protected by copyright law without permission

cyberbullying—when a person is tormented, threatened, harassed, humiliated, embarrassed, or otherwise targeted by another person using the Internet, interactive and digital technologies, or mobile phones

cyberspace—the online world of the Internet

dial-up—an Internet connection that is created using a modem to connect computers through standard phone lines

emoji—digital icons used to express emotions or depict places, items, or animals

floppy disks—small, thin, square cases with flexible disks that store data inside

go viral—to spread rapidly via the Internet, email, or other media

imperative—absolutely necessary

Internet service providers—companies that provide users with access to the Internet and other services such as website building and virtual hosting

malware—software that disrupts a computer's or device's normal way of functioning

paradigm shifts—major changes in how a process is accomplished

phishing—trying to obtain confidential information, typically by sending an email that looks as if it is from a legitimate organization, but contains a link to a deceptive website

plagiarism—act of using someone else's work without giving him or her credit for it

predators—people who use the Internet to locate and lure intended victims, especially children

privacy policy—a statement that declares a website's policy on collecting and releasing information

scammers—people intent on making quick profits through deception

spam—disruptive, unwanted messages

viruses— harmful, unauthorized programs that insert themselves into computer systems and then spread to other computers via shared networks

worms—harmful computer programs that replicate themselves to spread to other computers on the same network

Index

America Online (AOL), 4–5, 12

ARPANET, 6–8

Berry, Darrell, 5

bulletin board system (BBS), 10–11

CD-ROM, 8–9

chat room, 12

CompuServe, 4

copyright, 24–25

cyberbully, 28–29, 30, 32

emoji, 30

Facebook, 15, 19, 34–35, 38

FidoNet, 11

floppy disk, 8–9

Instagram, 15, 19

Internet, 4–10, 12, 14, 22, 26, 28, 30, 36

Internet Relay Chat (IRC), 12–13

Internet service providers (ISPs), 4, 10, 12

iVillage, 5

Jennings, Tom, 11

Koobface, 38

Leonsis, Ted, 5

LinkedIn, 14

packet switching, 6–7

password, 20, 40–41

phishing, 20

Pinterest, 15, 19

plagiarism, 24

scammer, 20–21, 36, 38

Sharkey, Tina, 5

Snapchat, 15, 19, 22

Tumblr, 15, 19

Twitter, 15, 19, 23, 34, 38

Walsh, John, 24

Yousafzai, Malala, 34

YouTube, 15, 19

Zuckerberg, Mark, 35

Check It Out!

Books

Boyd, Danah. 2014. *It's Complicated: The Social Lives of Networked Teens*. Yale University Press.

Gallo, Donald R. 1999. *No Easy Answers: Short Stories About Teenagers Making Tough Choices*. Laurel Leaf.

Myracle, Lauren. 2004. *ttyl*. Harry N. Abrams Publishing.

Video

Common Sense Media. "5 Social Media Musts for Teens." https://www.commonsensemedia.org/videos/5-social -media-musts-for-teens.

Websites

Internet Safety 101. http://internetsafety101.org.

Stopbullying.gov. http://www.stopbullying.gov.